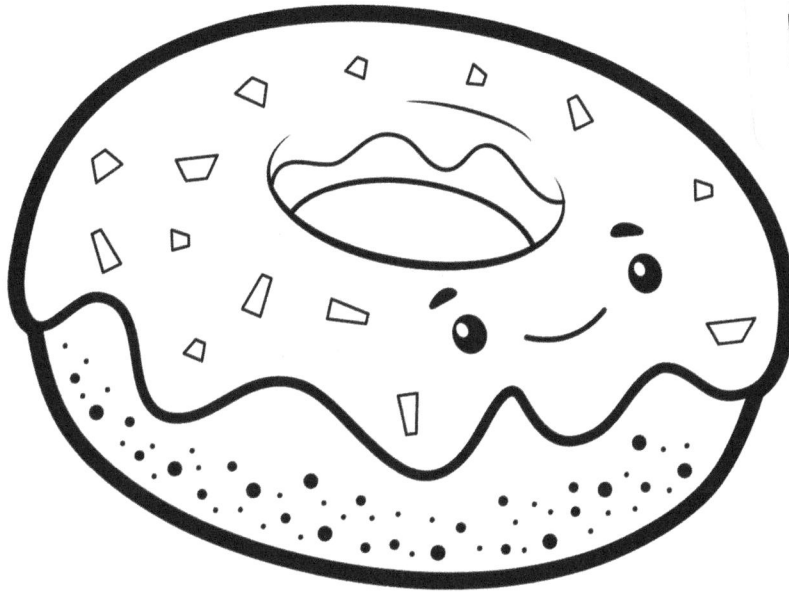

THIS COLORING BOOK BELONGS TO

_____

_____

BOLD AND EASY LARGE PRINT COLORING BOOK

COLOR TESTING

BEFORE YOU START COLORING

To enhance your coloring experience and prevent any ink bleed-through, this book features single-sided pages.

If you prefer using bold markers, we recommend placing a thicker piece of paper or cardboard behind the page you're coloring to provide extra protection for the page behind it.

Your enjoyment of coloring is our priority, and we hope these considerations contribute to a pleasant creative experience.

FOLLOW US

Scan the QR code to visit our social media pages.

Watch me color these designs—it's more fun than you'd expect!

I promise you'll laugh and get inspired!

TIKTOK

YOUTUBE

INSTAGRAM

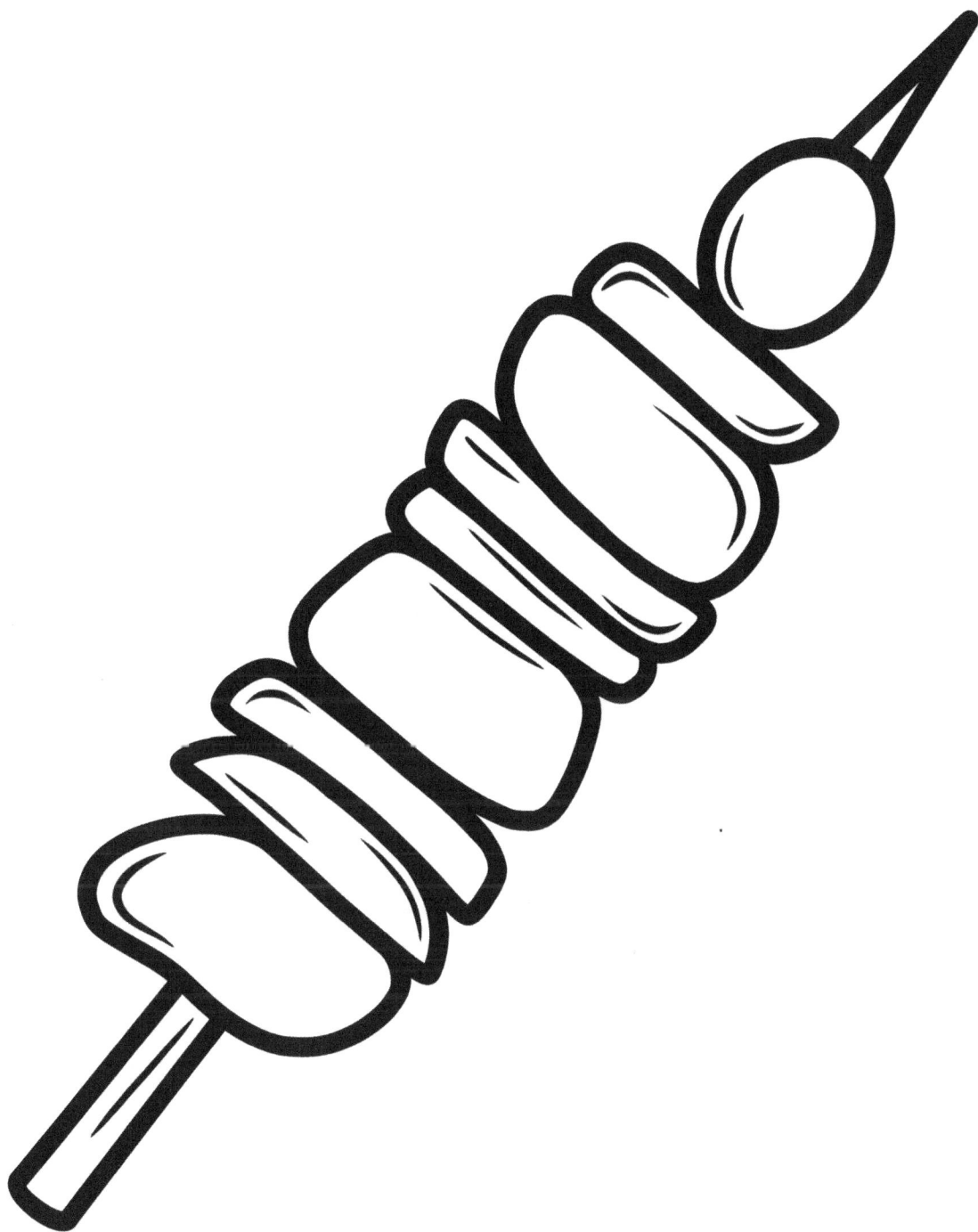

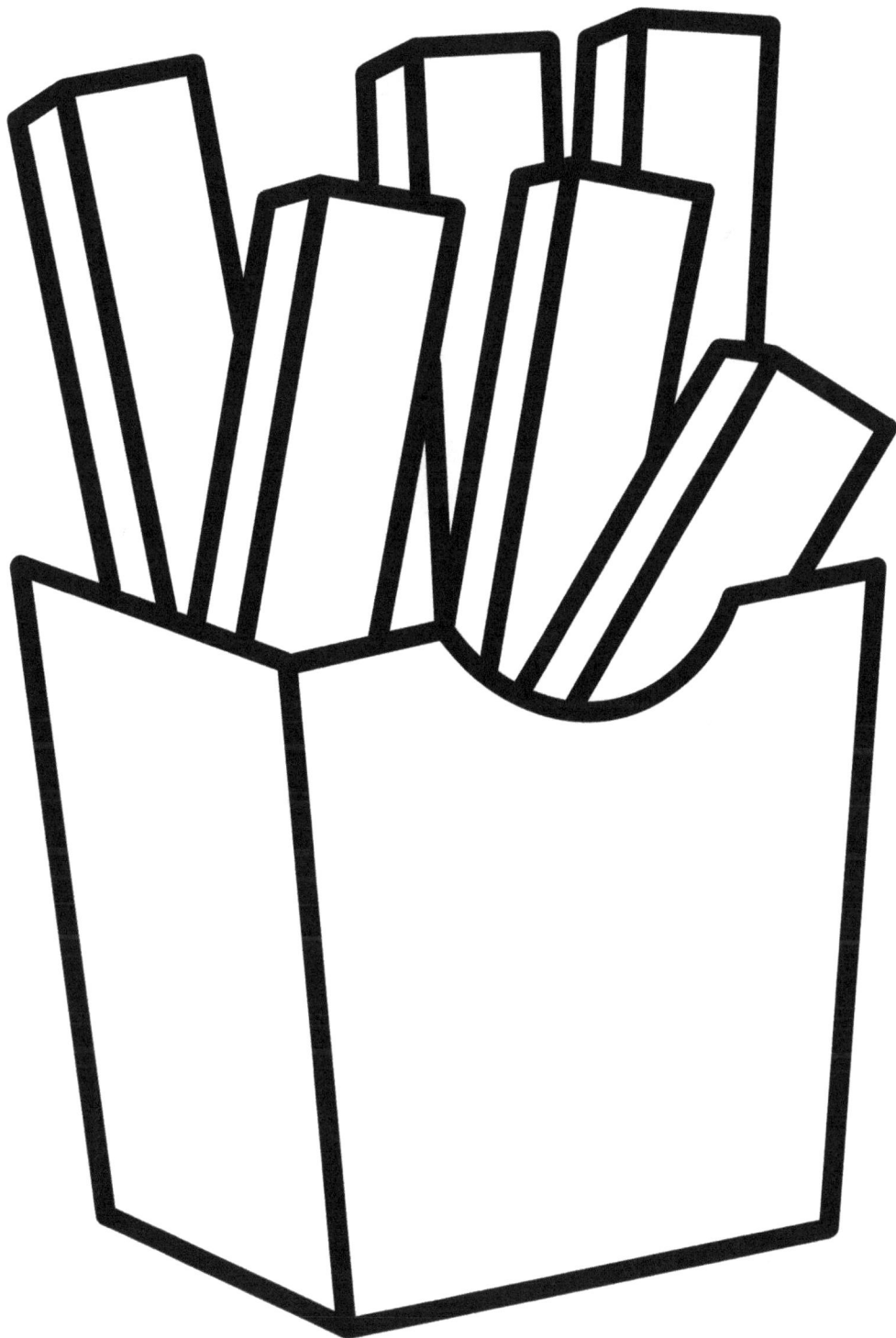

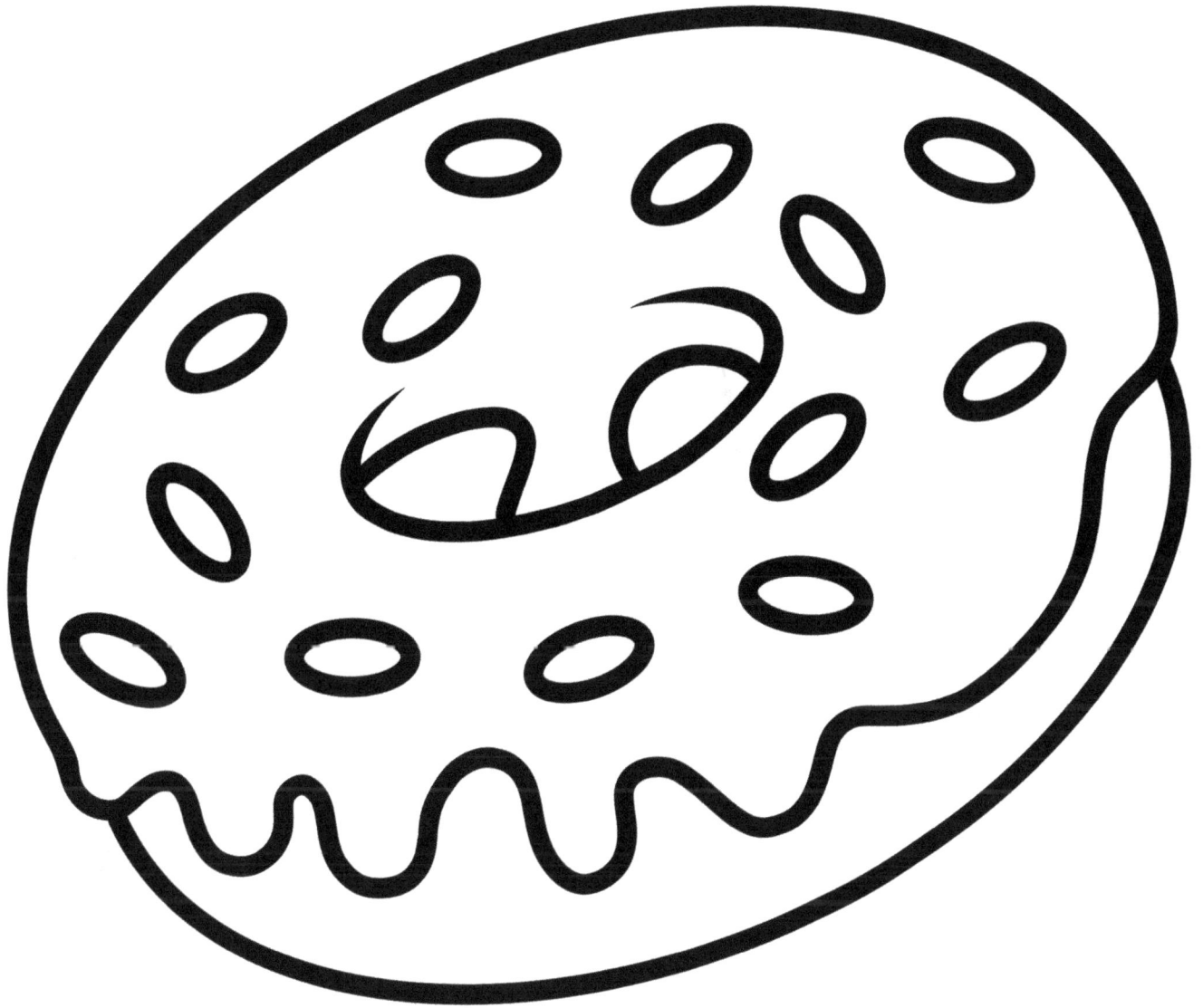

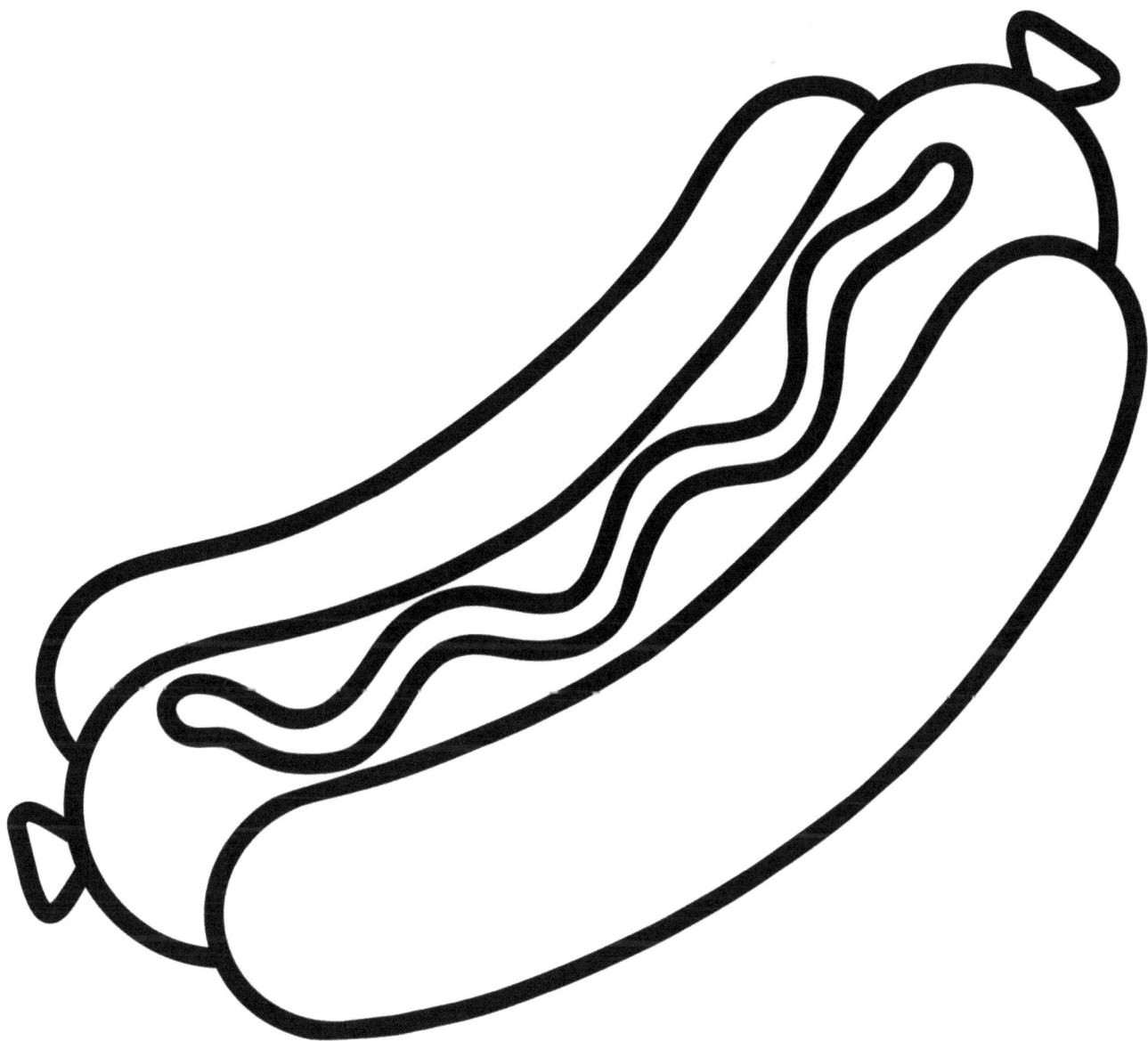

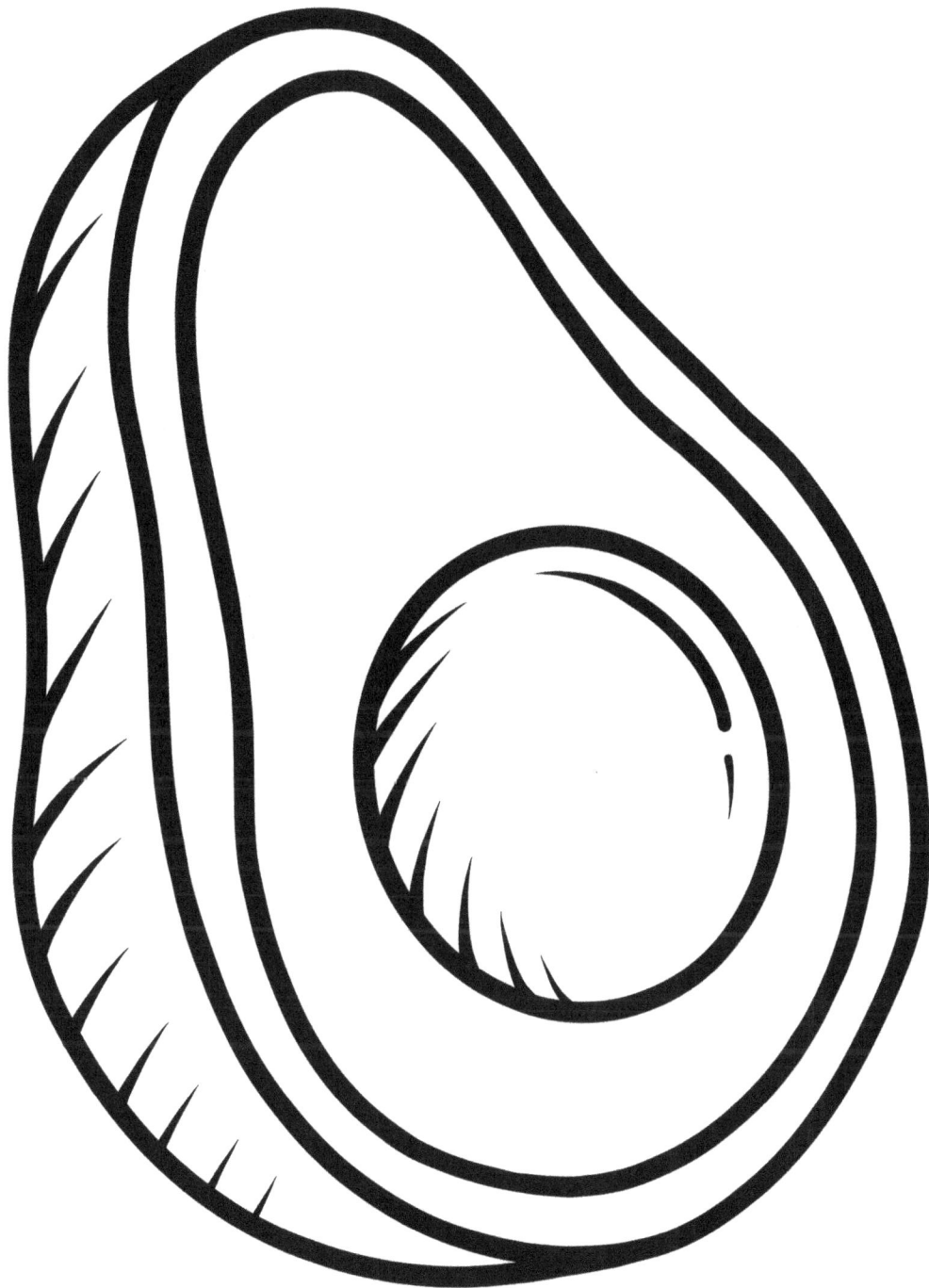

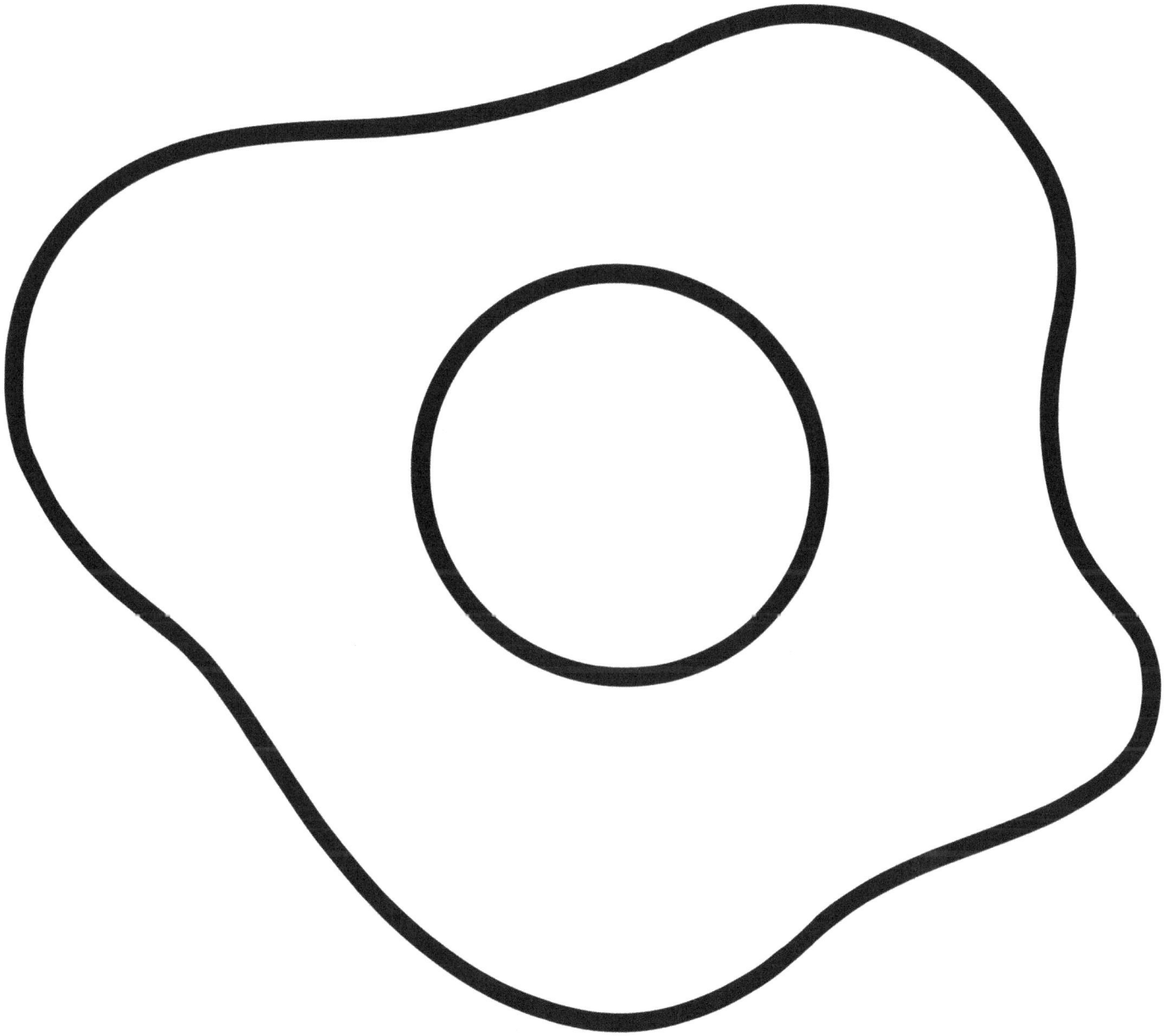

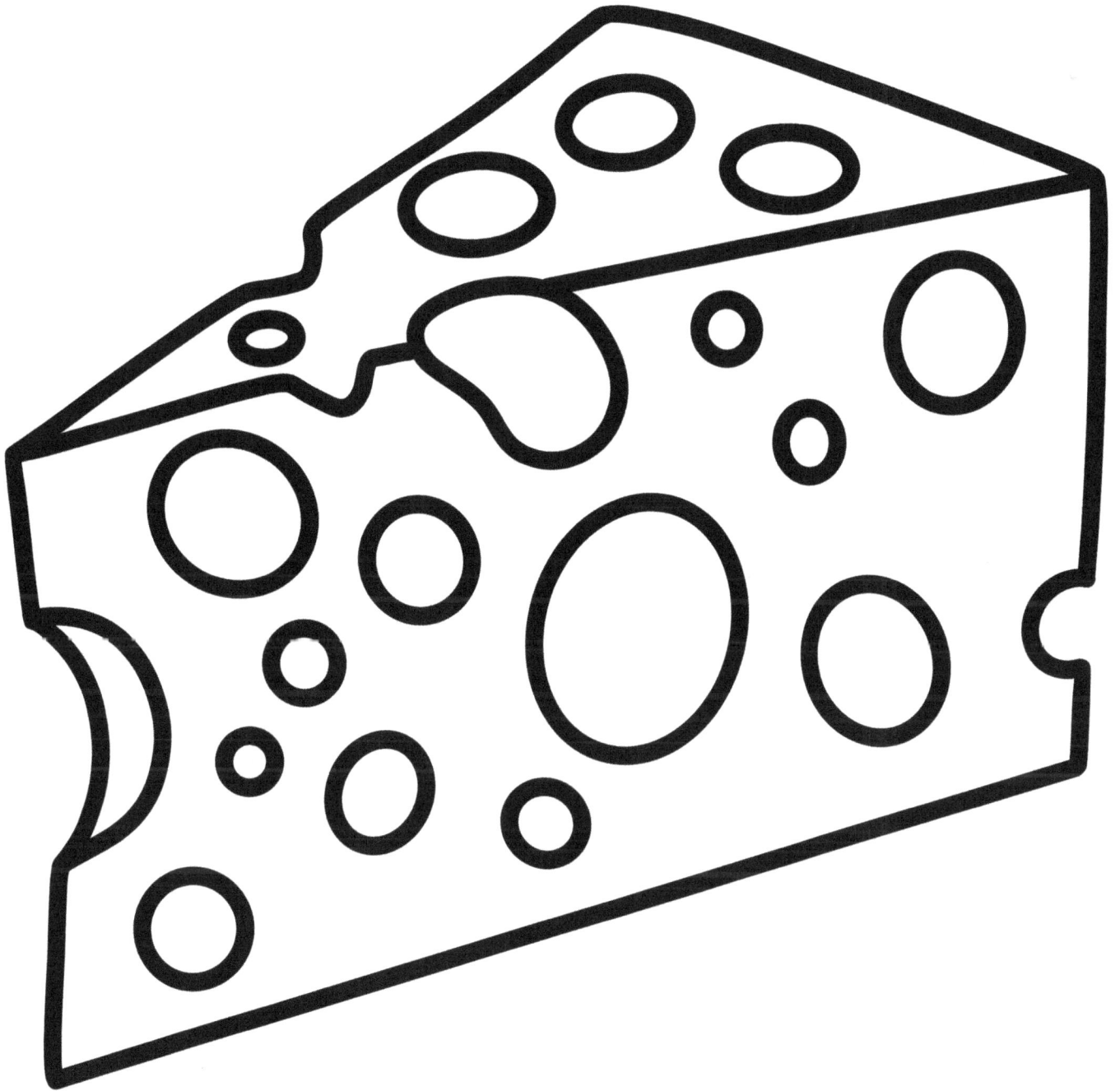

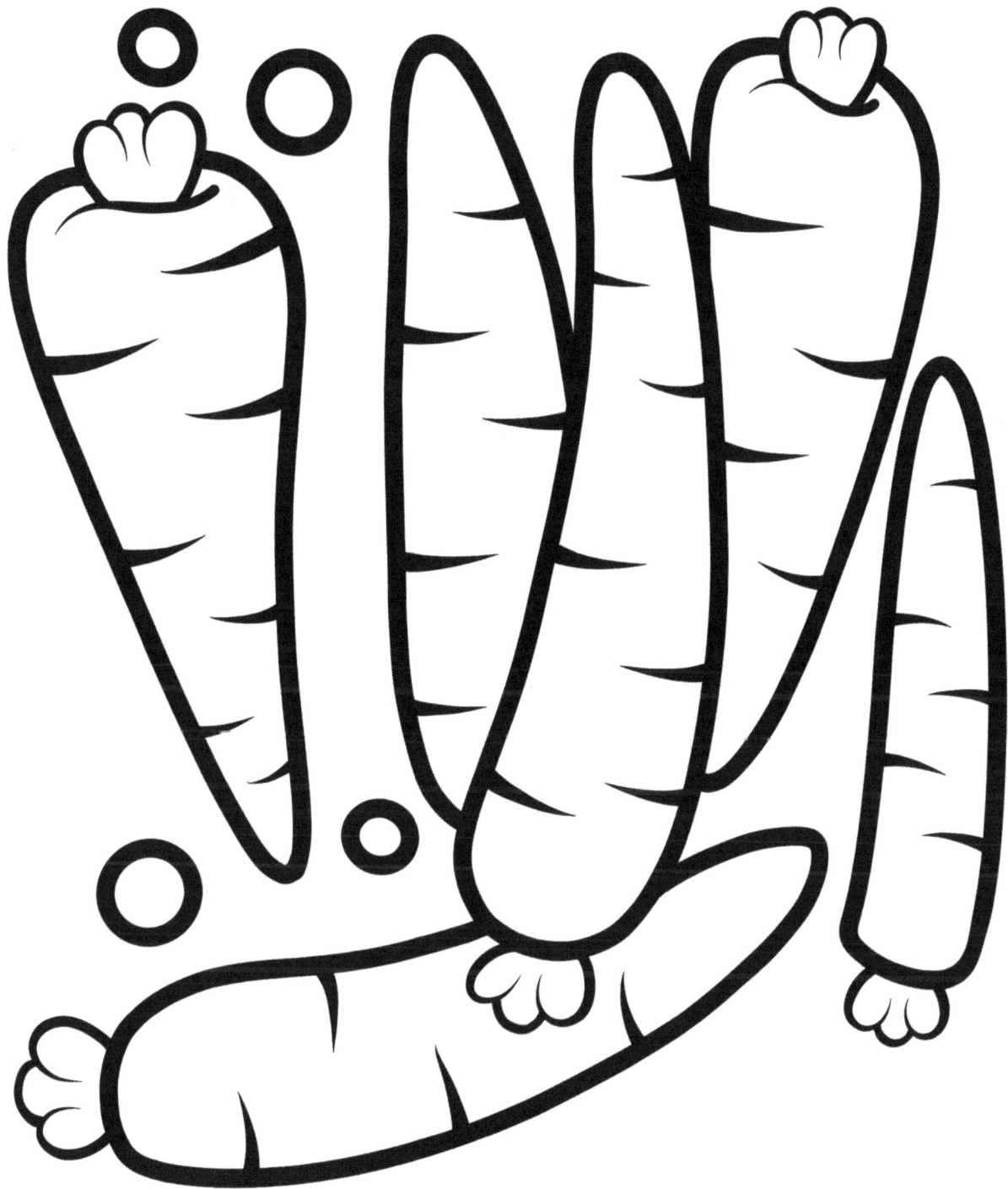

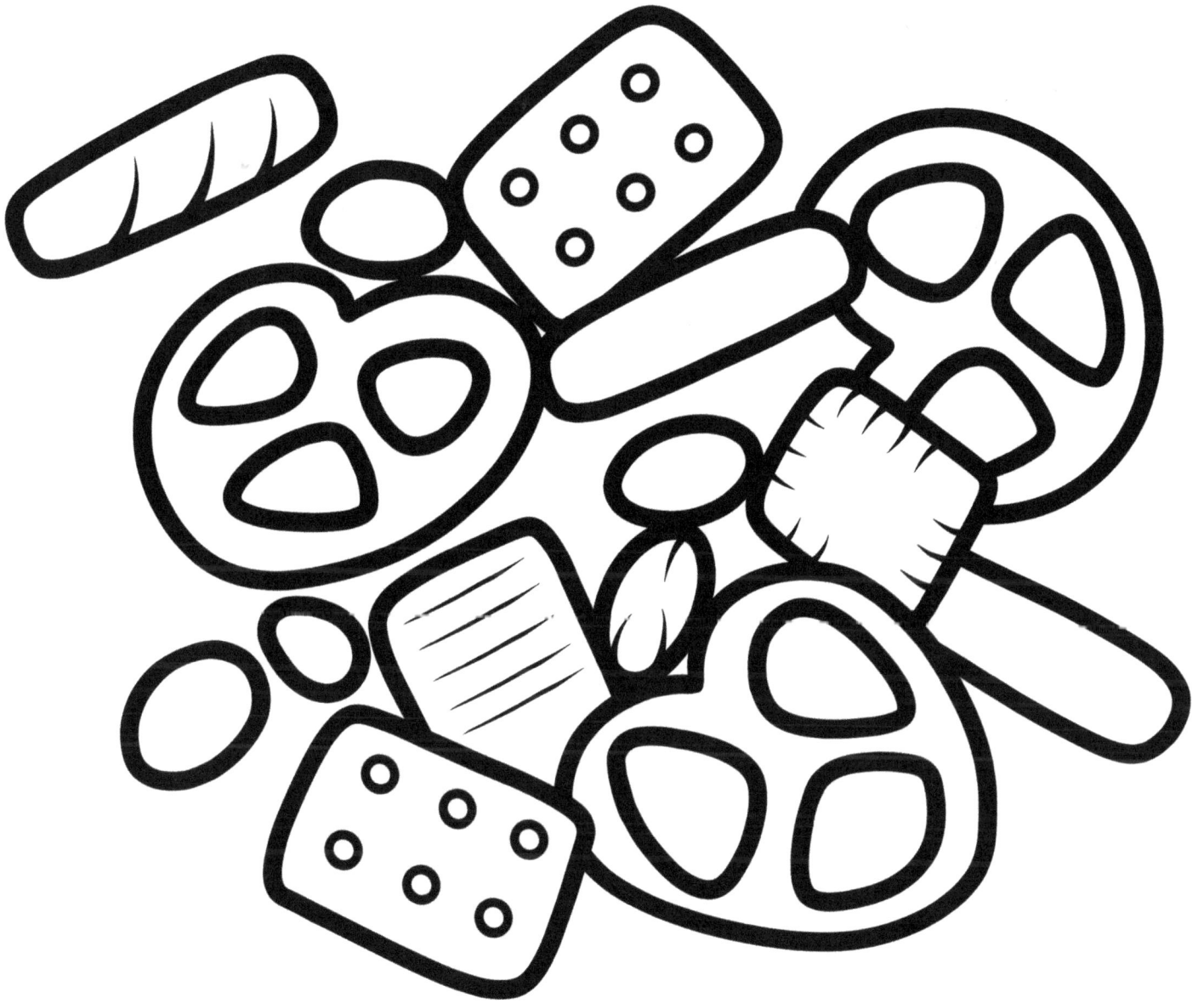

We Greatly Appreciate Your Valuable Feedback!

If you've found value in this book and would like to contribute to our growth, we kindly invite you to take a moment—just 30 seconds—to share your honest review on this book.

Your support truly means the world to us!

Scan the QR Code to Do Just That:

www.ingramcontent.com/pod-product-compliance
Lightning Source LLC
Chambersburg PA
CBHW080424030426
42335CB00020B/2583